MUSEUM GUIDES FOR Kids

Modern Art

Ruthie Knapp and Janice Lehmberg

Davis Publications, Inc.
Worcester, Massachusetts

Hello! I'm your tour guide, Rembrandt. This is a painting I did of myself. I have done lots of portraits of myself—about 100, in fact. In 1629 I finished this painting called *Artist in His Studio.* And *I'm* the artist, Rembrandt.

I've spent almost four hundred years trying to finish the painting on the easel. Do I ever need a break! I am going to hang up my palette with the one you see behind me on the wall and unlatch the door to your right. Then I can join you from time to time as you read this book. I would like to help you look at Modern art. After all, three centuries of painting have taught me a trick or two!

Rembrandt van Rijn, *Artist in His Studio,* ca. 1629.

© 2000 Janice G. Lehmberg and Ruth C. Knapp
Illustrations © John McIntosh of McIntosh Ink, Inc.

Design: Janis Owens

Printed in the United States of America
ISBN: 0-87192-548-6
10 9 8 7 6 5 4 3 2 1

Front cover: Salvador Dali, *The Persistence of Memory,* 1931. Oil on canvas, 9½ X 13" (24.1 x 33 cm). The Museum of Modern Art, New York. Given anonymously. Photograph © 2000 The Museum of Modern Art, NY. © 2000 Foundation Gala-Salvador Dali/VEGAP/Artists Rights Society (ARS), New York

CONTENTS

Modern Art

INTRODUCTION

Museum is a word like eggplant. It doesn't sound appealing. Children and adults often don't want to go to museums. We have written this book to help people of all ages enjoy new ways of looking at works of art, ways that make looking memorable and fun. Come with us and learn how to banish the **boring** and feature the **fun**.

Welcome to museum feet
"Museum feet" is that tired feeling you get after spending too much time in a museum. A case of museum feet makes you feel like saying: "This is boring. I could have done that myself. That's ugly. I'm hungry. I'm really hot. When can we sit down? What time is it?"

Studies of museum behavior show that the average visitor spends four seconds looking at an object. Children are more interested in smells, sounds, the "feel" of a place, and other people's faces than they are in looking at a work of art. Adults, sometimes unfamiliar with what they are seeing, cannot always answer children's questions. After a museum visit, it is only a short time before most everything is forgotten. Within a family or group of five, no one member will remember a shared looking experience the same way.

Word Wizard

Museum The word *museum* comes from the Greek word, *mouseion.* It means "a temple to the Muses." In Greek mythology, Zeus, king of the Greek gods, had nine beautiful daughters who never grew old. They were called the Muses and inspired creativity. Ancient Greek artists and writers asked the Muses to inspire them before they started work. We hope that you will look to a museum for inspiration, too!

Symbols to Help You Read This Book

Look closely at museum objects

A good idea

Additional information

Common questions

Avoiding Museum Feet

To avoid museum feet, try not to look at too many things. Studies show that young visitors get more out of a visit if they focus on seven (plus or minus two) objects—either five or nine objects. The fewer objects you see, the more you'll remember. One and a half hours is the ideal time to keep your eyes and mind sharp, and your feet happy!

Remember to take your time when looking at art.

"You can enjoy a work of art for as long as it takes to smell an orange. Then, to keep your interest, you have to do something more."
— SIR KENNETH CLARK,
BRITISH ART HISTORIAN, 1903–1983

This book is about doing something more.

What to bring
✓ Paper and pencil with eraser
✓ A plan of action
✓ A snack for the ride

Finding Your Way

A museum may feel big and confusing when you first arrive. If you are not familiar with the museum, find the Information Center or a guard. Ask for directions to the collection you want to see. Rooms in a museum are called **galleries.**

Museums are not the only places that have galleries. Prairie dogs, moles, and ants live in underground galleries. Old ships had galleries and so did forts.

Labels

Every work of art in a museum has a label. In the Modern art collection, a label might look like this:

Artist	**Reese Cycle**
Nationality, Life span	**(American 1953–)**
Title	***Mall Wandering,* 1991**
Medium	**Oil with feathers, paper, and receipts**
Acquisition information	**Gift of Modern Art Fund, 1999.02**

Accession number

Let's look at the label above. Reese Cycle is the artist. He is an American, and he was born in 1953 and is still living. The title of the work is *Mall Wandering*, and it was made in 1991. So, how old was the artist? (answer: 38 years old) He used oil paint along with other items on his canvas. The painting was bought for the museum with its Modern Art Fund in 1999. It was the second purchase that year.

Instruments/thingamajigs in museum galleries and cases

Some visitors are as interested in conservation equipment as they are in the objects on display. The *hygrometer* is a small dial that measures the humidity inside a display case. The *hygrothermograph* is a larger device that records the temperature and humidity of a museum gallery. This is often seen on the floor in a corner of the gallery.

Why can't we touch things? Fingers contain oils and salt which hurt fragile museum objects. Have you ever seen the mark your fingerprint leaves on a blackboard?

Your Turn to Smell the Orange

Form your first impression of the artwork. Let your eyes wander all over the surface. Absorb it. It is special, and it is yours. Taking time to look at a work of art is important because there is always more to it than first meets the eye.

Study this drawing carefully. What is it? Ask someone else what he or she thinks it is. Once you have taken a long look at a work of art, turn away from it. Wait a few seconds and turn back to look at it again. What is *new* this time?

Look at the Three Distances

When you look at a painting, think of three distances. The **foreground** is the part closest to you; the **middleground** is the area *between* what is closest to you and farthest away; the **background** is the part that is farthest away. In *Christina's World*, the foreground shows blades of grass and the figure of Christina. Do

Andrew Wyeth, *Christina's World*, 1948.

you see tire tracks leading to the farmhouse? This is the middle-ground. Beyond that, the background shows buildings and the sky. Remember after your first impression to check out the fore-ground, middle ground, and background. Looking at a painting this way helps you see things you might otherwise miss!

Maybe the painting you are looking at doesn't seem to have all three distances. It may resemble Rockwell's *The Connoisseur.* In *The Connoisseur,* the man in the foreground is trying to fig-ure out the painting in the background. Maybe he is searching for the three distances!

Norman Rockwell, *The Connoisseur.*

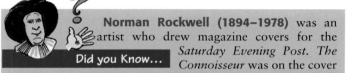

Norman Rockwell (1894–1978) was an artist who drew magazine covers for the *Saturday Evening Post. The Connoisseur* was on the cover in January of 1962, just when artists were creating paintings similar to the one the man is viewing! During the fifty-year period covered in this book, Norman Rockwell and Andrew Wyeth continued to work in their own styles, unmoved by the many innovations of modern art.

Look at Color

Colors can make us feel a certain way. There are warm and cool colors. Warm colors are reds, oranges, and yellows. They might make us think of fire. Restaurant owners often use red in their decor because it can make people feel hungry. Cool colors are blues, greens, and violets. They might make us think of glaciers and ice. Rooms in hot climates are often painted blue to look cool and fresh. Some colors get pushy in paintings. They like to show off. These colors stand out in a painting and grab your attention. They are usually warm colors like red. But white also can stand out, especially against a dull color. Other colors are quiet. In a painting, these are the darker colors.

Where do paint colors come from? In the past, painters used colors, known as pigments, found in bugs, plants, sea creatures, rocks, and earth. These are colors found in nature, and they can be used to make dyes. These days, most paints are chemically colored. In Modern art, acrylic paint is popular. It is plastic-based and water-soluble. It looks flatter than oil paint and is chemically colored.

Painting with pasta?

When an artist uses very thick paint on a canvas, it is called *impasto*. An easy way to remember this word is to think of pasta. Then think about strips of fettuccine or linguine, like thick brushstrokes, lying across a plate. The painter Hans Hofmann often used an impasto technique.

Hans Hofmann, *Goliath,* 1960. How many colors are there in this painting? Which color jumps out? Which is shy? hot? cold? quiet? noisy? Is one color dominant over the others? Try to imagine the painting without black.

Primary Colors

The three primary colors are **red, yellow,** and **blue.** All colors, except white and black, can be mixed from the three primary colors. But primary colors cannot be mixed from any other colors on earth. Look at the lower right of Hofmann's painting for the three primary colors.

Complementary Colors

Each primary color has a "best friend" color, called a complementary color. The complementary color makes red look redder, blue look bluer, and yellow look more yellow. To find the complementary color (or best friend) of a primary color, mix the other two primary colors together. Red's best friend is **green** (yellow + blue). Blue's best friend is **orange** (yellow + red). Yellow's best friend is **violet** (blue + red). Which, if any, complementary color is missing in Hofmann's painting? (**answer:** none are missing!)

Complementary Colors in Nature

Some complementary colors seem to occur naturally outside. Think of clay flower pots full of violet and yellow pansies, or red apples on green trees. Or blue butterflies with orange markings, and blue crocuses with orange centers. What about the blue embers of an orange flame?

Red-eyed tree frog.

Complementary Colors in Art

A Closer Look

Look again for three primary colors and their best friend complements in Hofmann's *Goliath*. They are red and green, yellow and violet, and blue and orange.

Qi Zhaijia, *Winter Landscape,* 1678.

Black and White

As museum-goers, we generally associate paintings with color. But some paintings have little color. Many Far Eastern paintings were made solely with black ink. The Chinese, however, refer to five shades of black because ink can be watered down to pale gray or thickened to deep black.

Scientists don't call black and white true colors, but imagine what paintings would be like without them. Artists use black to tone colors down and white to lighten them. Certain artists are famous for their use of black and white.

Look at Shape

Like colors, shapes in art can send messages. Shapes that are close together add energy to an artwork. Shapes that are far apart look more serene. Look for circles, squares, triangles, and ovals in works of art.

Look at Line

Lines can be diagonal, curved, vertical, and horizontal. Diagonal lines are action lines. Curved lines also lend a sense of motion. A vertical line is a strong, stable line. It gives a feeling of balance. A horizontal line is a quiet line.

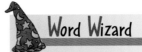

Word Wizard

Horizontal The word *horizontal* comes from *horizon,* the seemingly flat line where the earth meets the sky.

Look at Composition

Notes are arranged to make a musical composition and words are arranged to make a written composition. In art, colors, lines , and shapes are arranged to make a visual composition. Only the artist knows when the composition is just right.

Stuart Davis, *Hot Still Scape for Six Colors—7th Avenue Style,* 1940.

Looking at a composition is like meeting new people: some you like right away, and others take more time to get to know them!

What is Davis' composition about? What do you see that gives you that impression? (Some *possible* answers: It's about colors, shapes, crowds, a cluttered diamond laid diagonally, or maybe a room with a yellow vertical wall.)

Did you Know...

Stuart Davis said, "My abstract paintings *always* begin with something real, something I have just seen...remembered music...or read." He drew from the city life around him: police badges, lights, signs, and noises. How would you paint crowds and noise?

Look at Perspective

Artists use **perspective** to make a flat surface look as if it has depth. Look for tricks that artists use to create a sense of three-dimensional space on a two-dimensional surface.

- They make background objects smaller and less detailed because the eye sees less from a distance.
- They make background color lighter as it fades into space because the sky gets lighter as it gets farther away.
- They make parallel lines, like the sides of roads, come together to create deeper space.
- They layer the foreground, middleground, and background.

Look at Sculpture

A sculpture is an object that can be measured three ways. It has length, width, and thickness; or a front, a back, and sides—three dimensions. Since earliest times, people have made sculptures out of clay, bone, wood, and stone. Some sculptures are created by *carving away* material, like a pumpkin. In others, you *add* materials as you do when you make a snowman or a drip sand-castle. Modern sculptors such as Henry Moore, Barbara Hepworth, Alexander Calder, Isamu Noguchi, and David Smith have had the advantage of modern machinery, materials, and technology to help them make their large outdoor sculptures.

David Smith, *Cubi XVII*, 1963.

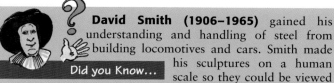

David Smith (1906–1965) gained his understanding and handling of steel from building locomotives and cars. Smith made his sculptures on a human scale so they could be viewed at eye-level and in an outdoor setting. He wanted the sun to add color to the steel.

To help you look at a sculpture, use the letters of the verb **SCULPT**.

S Surface, Scale, and Space Is the surface the same every-where? Is the scale life-size? How much space do you need to look at the sculpture?

C Condition Has the environment changed it?

U Unlike If it is a human, how is the sculpture **unlike** me? If it is an animal, how is it unlike the real animal?

L Light Is the sculpture the same color all over? Check for reflections.

P Place Did the sculptor make this sculpture for a particular place?

T Touch, Texture, Title If you could touch this sculpture, how would it feel? smooth? cold? bumpy? What material is it made of? What textures do you notice? What title did the sculptor give this piece? What title would you give it?

What else can I do to help me understand modern art?

• Take extra time to get your first impression, especially if you can't see perspective in the artwork.

• Remember, the artist is expressing *something*. It might be feelings about the paint itself and the joy of putting paint on canvas, or maybe it's a dream or a memory. The artist may want to push us, the viewers, into thinking hard about an event or idea related to our society or the environment.

- Let your eyes search the surface. In modern art, there are no rules on subject matter or surface materials! Check the surface of the work. Look at the texture. Check for brushstrokes and various shades of color. See if sand, paper, glitter, or other items have been added to the composition.
- Read the label. The title and date can give clues about what was going on outside the artist's window while she or he was working on the artwork.

Try your new looking skills on this painting by Morris Louis.

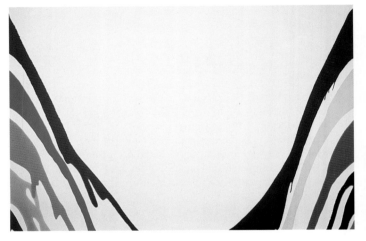

Morris Louis, *Delta Gamma,* ca. 1960.

Morris Louis (1912–1962) used acrylic paint directly on the canvas so that it was absorbed by cotton fibers. The canvas became the color! Sometimes, he tacked his canvas on the wall and poured the paint! Other times, he worked with the canvas on the floor. Either way, imagine keeping the colors away from each other *without* a paintbrush!

Did you Know...

Modern Art

The First Fifty Years

How are people and art alike? They are both constantly changing. In terms of art, there have been more changes in the twentieth century than in all other centuries combined! Modern artists reacted to the changes brought about by wars and technology. Many stopped copying the real world and turned to the imaginary world inside their heads.

Constantin Brancusi, *The Kiss,* 1916.

What marked the beginning of modern art in America? The Armory Show was like a clanging alarm, startling and awakening artists and the public. Seeing the unusual, groundbreaking styles of European artists made many American artists change their approach to their work.

Tired of being rejected? Many modern American artists, including a group called The Eight, or the Ash Can School, were tired of having their work rejected by art galleries, so they did something about it. Calling themselves the Association of American Painters and Sculptors, they (William Glackens, George Luks, Everett Shinn, John Sloan, Ernest Lawson, Arthur Davies, Robert Henri, and Maurice Prendergast and other American artists) invited innovative European artists to show their work in America for the first time—in the Armory Show. They wanted to exhibit their work along with the European art stars! They hoped to give American art "a new spirit."

Word Wizard

Soldiers and art An armory is a military storehouse or training center. Soldiers practiced marching in New York City's Sixty-Ninth Regiment Armory. For the Armory Show, which opened on February 17, 1913, the soldiers moved out and 1,500 works of art moved in. Screens were installed to break up the space. Potted pine trees were added to give the armory the smell of the forest.

Exterior View of the 69th Regiment Armory, 1913.

THE STARS ENTER

Here are two of the paintings from the Armory Show.

Marcel Duchamp, *Nude Descending a Staircase, No. 2,* 1912.

"An explosion in a shingle factory!"

It wasn't the subject of a nude that the public found shocking. It was the puzzling way in which she was presented. In what direction is she traveling? (**answer:** from top left to bottom right) The many overlapping images give the painting a sense of energy and movement.

Henri Matisse, *The Red Studio,* 1911.

"Madness was loose and so were the beasts."

When this painting was first shown, people thought it was outrageous and even crazy! Other paintings at the same exhibition included purple tree trunks, green striped faces, and blue hair. Thick layers of unexpected color soaked the art's simple shapes. One critic suggested that wild beasts must have painted the canvases! *Fauves,* French for wild beasts, was the name the group of artists proudly adopted. Their goal was to give pleasure and to free art from its past. The Fauves had a great impact on the use of color in twentieth-century art.

ART OOPS!

Success comes from failure Henri Matisse failed the entrance exam for the School of Fine Arts, the main art school in Paris. His teacher, Gustave Moreau, suggested he keep studying and then apply again later. He told the younger man to draw people in the streets of Paris and to copy the Louvre's masterpieces. But maybe the most important lesson Matisse learned was from Moreau's own paintings. Echoes of Moreau's use of delicate curves and curls taken from Islamic art can be seen in Matisse's *The Red Studio*. Matisse continued to be the master of the curve into the 1950s!

Stay Away!

Critics warned people to stay away from the Armory Show—the art on view there was thought to be too shocking! As a result, the crowds grew daily! Tens of thousands saw the exhibition during its month in New York. The show then moved to Boston and Chicago, where art students burned Henri Matisse and Constantin Brancusi in effigy! By the time the Armory Show closed, more than 300,000 people had visited it.

Why was the Armory Show so important? The American public was introduced to works by European avant-garde artists including Matisse, Picasso, and Brancusi. Collectors bought paintings and sculptures that would become the basis of museum collections. American artists experimented with European ideas they saw at the Armory.

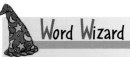

Word Wizard

The trendsetters The term **avant-garde** comes from a French word referring to the troops at the head of an army. It refers to people who are leaders in inventing new styles or techniques.

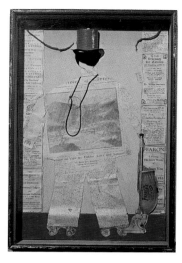

A critical note Art critics review artistic work and events. Because it is easier to refer to a group of similar paintings or a group of artists with similar concerns by one name, critics often labeled them. Artists frequently moved from one group to another.

Arthur Dove, *The Critic*, 1925.

A human bridge Modern art's key event was the Armory Show. There was also a key player. He was photographer Alfred Stieglitz (1864–1946), who became known as the father of modern photography. He had a tiny studio at 291 Fifth Avenue in New York. It was nicknamed 291. Stieglitz invited European and American avant-garde artists to show their work there. It was the site of art shows for twenty years.

Alfred Stieglitz, *The Steerage*, 1907.

Now let's travel the road through the first fifty years of modern art. To break up the trip, we have named the stops along the way:

Emoting Expressionists
Confusing Cubists
Fearless Futurists
Daring Dadaists
Super Surrealists

Awesome Abstractionists
Revealing Realists
Action Artists
Popular Pop Artists
Marvelous Minimalists

EMOTING EXPRESSIONISTS

1905–1930s

How are you feeling? Some of the first modern artists are called Expressionists. These artists expressed, or showed, feelings through their art. To do this, they used strong lines, energetic brushstrokes, sharp angles, distorted shapes, and clashing colors. They were not trying to make things look real or natural in their artworks.

Where were the Expressionists? The Expressionist movement began in two cities in Germany. One group came together in Dresden where they drank tea. The other met in Munich where they drank coffee.

The tea drinkers. In Dresden, the tea-drinking Expressionists were led by an artist named Ernst Ludwig Kirchner. The group gathered in an old shop where they built furniture and took painting lessons. Their goal was to link the past with the future in their art, so they called themselves *Die Brücke* (dee brew-ka) which means "the Bridge." The Bridge was formed in 1905.

The coffee drinkers. In 1911, artists Wassily Kandinsky and Franz Marc founded a second Expressionist group in Munich. Kandinsky had been told he could not show his paintings at an exhibition because they did not have a subject. In response, he and Marc formed a group that they named *Der Blaue Reiter* (der blah-uh ri-teh), or "the Blue Rider," simply because they loved the color blue and horse riders! The Blue Rider artists used color and shape to show emotion in their artwork. Their paintings are more cheerful than those of the Bridge.

Off the Wall with

Ernst Ludwig Kirchner
(1880–1938)

Ernst Ludwig Kirchner studied to be an architect, but preferred painting and making woodcuts. He is best known for his woodcuts. Kirchner and the Bridge artists wanted to create art that was different from the Impressionist style, which was popular at the time. Kirchner tried to capture the noise and motion of German life. His style of painting includes strong, straight lines and harsh colors. After the beginning of World War I, Kirchner was so shocked at all the destruction that he stopped painting for a long time. When he returned to painting, he created only landscapes.

A   Closer Look

- Notice your first impressions. What is this artwork about?
- Look at the lines. In what direction are they going?
- Check the faces in the crowd. What does the color say about the feelings of these people? (gloomy)
- Think about how color is used to produce a feeling in this street scene.

Ernst Ludwig Kirchner, *Street Scene: Two Ladies in the Street,* 1922.

What did the German government think of Kirchner's Expressionist art? The German government didn't like Kirchner's style of art. They thought he was a bad influence. In 1937, the government confiscated 639 of Kirchner's works. Many of them were never seen again.

Off the Wall with

Wassily Kandinsky
(1866–1944)

When he was a thirty-year-old lawyer, Kandinsky visited an Impressionist art exhibition. He saw Claude Monet's paintings of haystacks, and realized it was possible to express feelings in paint without showing a recognizable object. Kandinsky decided to abandon his law career to become a painter. He left Russia to study at Munich's Royal Academy. Kandinsky's paintings show feelings and moods, not people, places, or things. He uses different shades of a color and brushstrokes of varying widths to express himself.

After graduating from the Academy, Kandinsky traveled to Italy, Tunisia, and France before returning to Munich and co-founding the Blue Rider group with Franz Marc. During World War I, the Blue Rider disbanded. After the war, Kandinsky taught at the Bauhaus in Germany. When Hitler closed the Bauhaus in 1933, Kandinsky fled to France, where he spent the rest of his life painting and writing.

ART SCOOP

Seeing sound *"The need for objects has no place in my paintings."* —Kandinsky, 1910
Kandinsky thought paintings should be heard and sounds should be seen.

The Bauhaus In 1922, artisans, painters, architects, engineers, and sculptors began gathering in Dresden, Germany, at a place they called the Bauhaus. The word *bauhaus* is from the German word *bauthutte* which means "house of the master mason." The Bauhaus was a series of connected buildings that housed classrooms, workshops, cafeterias, and dormitories. Its purpose was to bring all the arts together in one place. Students at the Bauhaus combined art and the beauty of machinery in everyday things.

Look for artworks by other artists who taught or studied at the Bauhaus and check off the ones you find.
- ○ **Paul Klee**
- ○ **Josef Albers**
- ○ **Piet Mondrian**

- What musical instruments do you imagine playing or hearing as you look at the composition below?
- Does this composition make you want to dance fast?
- Look around your museum for a painting with colors and shapes but no recognizable objects. What mood do you think it shows?

Wassily Kandinsky, *Panel for Edwin R. Campbell No. 3*, 1914.

Bluegrass, and it's not Kentucky! In Hitler's time, government officials did not trust Expressionist artists, who portrayed skies as green or grass as blue. They thought these artists were ill and dangerous. "After all," they thought, "what kind of person thinks grass is blue?" The Expressionists were allowed to exhibit their work in a show called "730 Horrors," in a poorly lit warehouse next to the main German House of Art. No one under eighteen was allowed to attend the exhibit, and adults were allowed entry only every three minutes. Despite these strict rules, thousands of people waited in line to see this show—many more than attended an approved exhibition next door! Of course, these paintings were not horrible at all, just different from anything painted before.

Did you Know...

Confusing Cubists

1907–1920s

How many sides does a cube have? Six. If you painted a cube sitting on a table, how many sides would you include in your painting? If you showed exactly what you see, you would show three sides: the top and two sides. In the early 1900s, some artists decided to show all the sides of an object at once in their artwork, not just the ones they could actually see. How did they do this? They drew all the different views of an object and then rearranged them so that they tilted, overlapped, and shaded each other. The artists who worked in this style are called Cubists because their ideas were founded on looking at a simple cube and portraying all the views of it using a combination of geometric shapes.

Who invented Cubism? Pablo Picasso and Georges Braque invented Cubism in the summer of 1909. They shared a studio, ideas, and still-life objects on a table—glasses, musical instruments, and bottles—to create monochromatic (one-color) paintings of the shapes from all angles. Braque recalled, "We were like two mountaineers roped together." Independently, they had already been using sharp shapes and angles in their work. Together, they developed new ways to make art.

Puzzling Cubist paintings require viewers to look very carefully, almost like putting the pieces of a puzzle together. Often, the title of an artwork will give clues to the puzzle.

Did Americans paint Cubist paintings? The only American artist to completely adopt the Cubist style was Max Weber. Cubism influenced many other American painters in various ways. Keep an eye open for signs of Cubism (geometric shapes and monochromatic color schemes) in your museum.

 Why is Picasso so famous? He created tens of thousands of works of art from paintings and sculptures to ceramics, costumes, set designs, and poetry. His work spans every major art period in this book!

Off the Wall with

Pablo Picasso
(1881–1973)

Pablo Picasso was one of the most influential and well-known modern artists. Born in Spain into an artist's family, he took art lessons from an early age and had his own studio by the age of fifteen.

Picasso constantly experimented with drawing and colors. His life's work reveals how he moved through distinctly different periods in his life. You may have heard of Picasso's Blue Period. This refers to a time when he used only shades of blue in his artwork. Later, he used only shades of pink or rose. This is called his Rose Period. Picasso liked to show women in his art. Some say that he went from his sad Blue Period to the warmer Rose Period because he fell in love for the first time.

Picasso in front of Guernica, July 1937.

Stronger than words Picasso was devastated by the Spanish Revolution and the bombing of a town called Guernica in 1937. The tragedy became the subject of a mural he made for the Spanish Pavilion at the World's Fair in Paris. This mural was twenty-five feet long and eleven feet high! The painted images were so powerful and emotional that everyone who saw them was reminded of the horrible things humans do in wartime. The mural, *Guernica*, became an international statement against war.

Pablo Picasso

Pablo Picasso, *Three Musicians*, 1921.

A   Closer Look

- Look hard. How many people can you see in this painting?
- Describe the three musicians. What colors and shapes did the artist use to show these people?
- Can you find a guitar in the painting? Try to find a dog.

Speaking of dogs Picasso said, "People who try to explain pictures are usually barking up the wrong tree." What do you think he meant by that?

ART OOPS!

Beware of falling sculpture At a party in Picasso's studio, things got a little out of control. Gertrude Stein, an art collector and writer, told a story about two huge statues being jostled, and Georges Braque rushing to catch them just as they were about to topple over on guests. He saved the guests...and the sculptures, too!

On the Floor with

Jacques Lipchitz
(1891–1973)

Jacques Lipchitz was born in Latvia and moved to America when he was ten years old. As an adult, he studied art in Paris where he spent time with artists Picasso and Diego Rivera. Lipchitz is known for his stone and bronze sculptures. His work spans many styles but his Cubist work with overlapping straight lines is shown here. In all his work, there is a sense of stretching or pulling.

Lipchitz returned to America during World War II. The effects of both world wars influenced him to include religious and mythological subjects in his sculpture.

A Closer Look

- Can you find the guitar in this sculpture? Think about the parts of a guitar. Now look again. Find the round sound hole of the guitar.
- Try to imagine the rhythm of the light and dark areas in the sculpture. How might a guitar player move?
- Imagine the music this musician might be playing right now.

Jacques Lipchitz, *Man With a Guitar*, 1915.

Here are some other Cubist artists whose artwork you might find in your museum. Check off the ones you find.

○ **Fernand Léger**
○ **Juan Gris**
○ **Alexander Archipenko**
○ **Raymond Duchamp-Villon**

FEARLESS FUTURISTS

1909–1923

How do you draw the speed and energy of a turning bicycle wheel? Futurists painted objects as they might look when they are moving. For example, Futurists would paint a person running or machinery grinding. To turn energy into a painting, they used overlapping images and repeated lines. Their subjects were what they saw when they looked around them, which at that time included World War I. Futurists worked in Italy while the Cubists were working in France.

How did the Futurists study running? English photographer Eadweard Muybridge took the first-ever series of stop-action photographs. His work influenced the Futurists' understanding of movement by showing it one frame at a time. For example, it made it possible to see various leg positions of a fast-moving dog.

Giacomo Balla, *Dynamism of a Dog on a Leash,* 1912.

ART SCOOP

Love of danger Usually art critics name a trend in the art world, but the Futurists named themselves! They wanted to break away from Italy's old masters and become the leaders of contemporary art. "We shall sing the love of danger, energy, and boldness," the Futurists announced. They climbed to the top of a bell tower and flung announcements to the crowd below!

Off the Wall with

Joseph Stella
(1877–1946)

Stella's family moved to New York from Italy when he was young. He studied at the New York School of Art. One of his first jobs was drawing steel mills for a magazine. He loved the idea of industry, but missed Italy and its climate. So, he returned. He met a founder of Futurism, Gino Severini, who made a major impression on him. When Stella sailed back to New York in 1912, he joined Stieglitz's 291 and lived near the huge, steel Brooklyn Bridge, which became a subject of many paintings. Stella uses repeated shapes and sharp angles to change motion and energy into art.

Joseph Stella, *Battle of Lights, Coney Island,* 1913.

- What is going on in this painting?
- What do you see that makes you say that?

A Closer Look

- Check for the curving lines of a roller coaster.
- Look for a triangle near the high center. (Tower of Lights)
- Check your museum for paintings that look full of motion with twisting, overlapping, or jagged lines.

Joseph Stella

Stella sees the light While Stella was on a bus going to Coney Island, he could see the bright Tower of Lights out the window. As he drew closer, he saw the swirling rides and the whirling Ferris wheel. He sensed the overall throbbing of the yellow lights, which you can see in his painting! *Battle of Lights, Coney Island* was in the Armory Show.

Coney Island Steeplechase Park.

Where have all the rabbits gone? Coney Island is a little strip of land in Brooklyn, New York. Its name, Coney, comes from the Dutch word for rabbits. It really isn't an island anymore because the water on one side was filled in to connect it to the mainland. It is famous for two reasons. First, explorer Henry Hudson landed there in 1609. Second, Coney Island is a seaside resort where as many as a million people a day go to have fun. Many of them play carnival games or go on the rides in the amusement park.

Did you Know...

On the Floor with

Umberto Boccioni
(1882–1916)

By the time Boccioni was twenty-six, he had traveled from his home in Italy to France and Russia, written a book and magazine articles, and helped create the Futurists! Although he was a painter, he is known as Italy's best early-twentieth-century sculptor. Many of his sculpture subjects were humans as they moved through space. He showed strength and motion by distorting or emphasizing their muscles.

Umberto Boccione, *Unique Forms of Continuity in Space*, 1913.

A Closer Look

- If this sculpture were wired for sound, what would you hear?
- Try to find the figure's feet. Note how it is grounded, or attached to its base.
- Check the "air" surrounding the figure. Can you see the bronze flutter as the figure pushes aside the air in its path?
- Look in your museum for motion in sculpture. How did the sculptor create motion? (diagonals, sharp edges, overlapping)

Here are some other Futurist artists whose work you might see in your museum. Check off the ones you find.

- ○ **Giacomo Balla**
- ○ **Gino Severini**
- ○ **Carlo Carrà**
- ○ **Mikhail Larionov**
- ○ **Natalya Goncharova**

DARING DADAISTS

1916–1923

Have you ever known someone who was against this, against that, and anti-everything else? A couple of people with that attitude met in 1916 in Zurich, Switzerland. They decided to be anti-tradition. They wanted to lead a revolt that would shake up and shock everyone's idea of art, literature, and music. Some people say they chose their name by opening a French dictionary and pointing to a word at random. The word was *dada,* which means "hobbyhorse" or "rocking horse."

Why did the Dadaists want to change art? Upset and disgusted by the effects of World War I, Dadaists wondered, "Why spend time creating when things can be blown apart by war?" They wanted to be free from the past and its values. The Dadaists held public performances of noise music. They wrote poetry by drawing words from a hat, and then recited the poems by shrieking the words at the top of their lungs. Dadaist ideas spread to Germany, France, and America. They believed that "Art with a capital A is everywhere," even in ready-made things.

Off the Wall with

Marcel Duchamp
(1887–1968)

French artist Marcel Duchamp created some paintings with geometric shapes, like *Nude Descending a Staircase No. 2* (page 19), but he is best known for his "ready-mades." All he did to create ready-mades was to choose ordinary objects and set them up as art! His ready-mades included a shovel, a hat stand, a bottle rack, and a bicycle wheel. He believed art was all around us.

After moving to New York with his Dadaist friend, Francis Picabia, Duchamp continued to fascinate and shock people with his art. Many critics think Duchamp had as much effect on modern artists as Picasso or Matisse.

Marcel Duchamp, *Bicycle Wheel*, 1951.

A Closer Look

- What is your first impression? Remember, art is everywhere!
- Think of an everyday object such as a sneaker. Don't think about how it is used.
- Now think of its lines, color, shape, and overall look.
- Put it on a stand. It's YOUR Dadaist art: a ready-made!

ART SCOOP

A dog's day Duchamp submitted a work called *Fountain* to the New York Independents Exhibition in 1917. He signed it R. Mutt, which was the name of a manufacturer of bathroom fixtures. The judges for the show hid *Fountain* behind a wall, probably because it was a porcelain urinal! Duchamp wrote them a letter in his magazine *The Blind Man*. He noted that Mr. Richard Mutt had sent the required six dollars with a piece of work that was never exhibited. He continued that his *Fountain* was seen every day in plumbing stores and wasn't immoral. Also, it didn't matter that Mr. Mutt hadn't made it; it only mattered that he *chose* it. "He created a new thought for this object." Duchamp believed the idea of carefully choosing an ordinary object was enough to call it art!

Making Choices Francis Picabia was a devout Dadaist. He was given the best art education. He studied his grandfather's collection of old master paintings and copied them perfectly. Then he sold the originals to raise money to buy more stamps for his collection!

Did you Know...

On the Floor with

Jean Arp
(1887–1966)

Arp studied art in Paris and then showed his work with the Blue Rider artists and the Expressionists. Later, he became a founder of the Dada movement. Throughout his life, he wrote, painted, made engravings, designed tapestries (woven pictures), and made collages. He is best known for his sculpture. He believed art is within nature and people the way a seed is within an apple. His forms are soft and rhythmic with a feeling of being alive. As with so many artists, Arp's style changed with time, and he soon became involved in Surrealism, the next chapter!

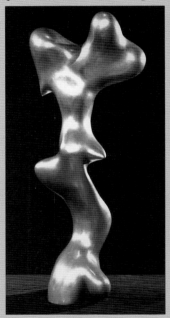

Jean Arp, *Growth*, 1938.

A Closer Look

- Notice how the curves push upward as if the piece is growing.
- Check your museum for a free-form work. Walk around it.
- Which side is your favorite?

Here are some other Dadaist artists whose work you might see in your museum. Check off the ones you find.

- ○ Kurt Schwitters
- ○ George Grosz
- ○ Man Ray
- ○ Morton Livingston Schamberg
- ○ Hannah Hoch

SUPER SURREALISTS

1924–1930s

Do you ever wonder where your dreams come from? Scientists say they come from a part of the mind called the "subconscious." The subconscious is like a whole little world inside our heads. At night, when we sleep, it awakens! Some artists painted their dreams.

These artists wanted to write and paint about what they called the "super truth" that appeared in their subconscious. They named themselves Surrealists, combining the French word *sur,* meaning "over" or "above," and *real.* Sometimes they painted recognizable or real objects in a very strange environment. These weird and incongruous juxtapositions create a mood or feeling of fantasy or unreality.

I think this painting is weird. Why should I keep looking at it? Surrealist paintings are full of surprises. Just keep looking, and eventually you may begin to get it.

ART SCOOP

Pictures in the floor! Max Ernst (1891–1976) was the first Surrealist. One day in his hotel room he was staring at the hardwood floors. He saw swirling images in the grain in the wood the way you can sometimes see images in the clouds in the sky. He grabbed paper and pencil and fell to his knees. He placed the paper over the board and rubbed it with a pencil to copy the images onto the paper. Later, he used tree bark to create *frottages,* which means rubbing in French.

Off the Wall with

Salvador Dali
(1904–1989)

Dali was born in Spain and was a wild, precocious, and spoiled child. He was expelled from almost every art school he attended! His first painting, a still life with three lemons, sold when he was six years old! His painting style could be Classical, Fauve, or Impressionistic. He is best known for what he called "hand-painted dream photographs." He felt he could step into a fantasy or the subconscious world anytime he wanted. He created movies, wrote books, designed stage sets and costumes, and staged events.

A Closer Look

- Let your eyes wander around this painting. What is going on? What is it about?
- What looks real? What doesn't?
- Check the middleground and background. What else do you notice?
- Look in your museum for familiar objects painted in an unusual way.

More Cheese? Salvador Dali painted a world where anything is possible. Historians say that he created this painting after eating runny Camembert cheese, which had given him a headache.

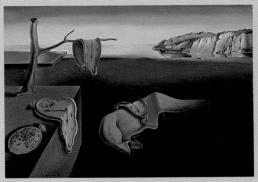

Salvador Dali, *The Persistence of Memory*, 1931.

Word Wizard

Salvador means "the savior." Dali thought his mission was to save the art of painting in the twentieth century. Dali made a chart to rank the best artists in history. He placed himself third, behind Leonardo da Vinci and the Dutch master Jan Vermeer.

Diving into art Dali did outrageous things, like giving a lecture with one foot soaking in a basin of mule milk or attending a meeting with a thermometer under his tongue so he was unable to talk. Another time, his actions almost killed him. He showed up at an art opening wearing a diving helmet. He had intended to read a love letter to his wife when he suddenly started shaking. Most people thought the shaking was part of his presentation, but one guest guessed that Dali might be suffocating. He rushed forward, removed the helmet, and saved him!

Off the Wall with

Joan Miró
(1893–1983)

When Miró joined the Surrealists, he was so poor he was eating only a few dried figs a day. He painted in a semiautomatic way, letting the paintbrush journey about the canvas more or less on its own. His forms were from his childhood memories. Throughout his life, his art changed, and he made wood constructions, murals, and ceramics. He is known for his use of color and simple shapes that look as if they might be from outer space.

Joan Miró

Joan Miró, *The Harlequin's Carnival*, 1924–25.

A Closer Look

- Just look at it. Keep looking.
- What is going on? Where is it happening? Check the two shades of brown creating a horizontal line. Maybe it's a floor and a wall.
- Are there any hints of people?
- Look in your museum for a painting that is unusual— totally unlike anything you've ever seen. Give it time to unfold for you.

On the Floor with

Alberto Giacometti
(1901–1966)

Giacometti was born in Switzerland where his father was a leading Post-Impressionist painter. Giacometti later moved to Paris where he met Miró and wrote poetry for Surrealist publications. He is known for his very thin bronze sculptures in which he reduced animal and human form to its bare minimum. Some of his standing people are so small and thin that they can fit in a matchbox!

Alberto Giacometti

Alberto Giacometti,
Dog, 1951.

• How is this different from real dogs you have seen?

• What has the sculptor done to suggest the difference? (skeleton-like, head downward, sharper angles, sad-looking ears, weak back)

• Look for a piece of sculpture in your museum. Check its base to see how it is attached.

Did you Know... On a rainy day, Giacometti took a walk and saw a dog. The soaked animal reminded him of himself because he, too, was hungry and wet. He went home and began sculpting *Dog*.

Did any European artists ever travel to America? Yes, they did—often because they wanted to escape their war-torn countries. They taught art, exhibited their works, and made a huge impact on American artists and museum visitors. Some of the artists visiting America during this time were Duchamp, Ernst, Dali, and Miró.

Here are some other Surrealist artists whose work you might see in your museum. Check off the ones you find.
○ **Man Ray**
○ **Joseph Cornell**
○ **Arshile Gorky**
○ **Giorgio de Chirico**

AWESOME ABSTRACTIONISTS

1910–1925

You might be thinking, "Haven't I already been looking at abstract art?" The answer is: Yes! There are many kinds of abstract art, but it is all alike in two ways: It requires thought on the part of the viewer, and it involves little or no copying of the world around us. Color, lines, shapes, and feelings are more important to abstract artists than imitating nature.

 Where do artists get their ideas? Artists study other artists. That is why many American artists (Arthur Dove, John Marin, Max Weber, Marsden Hartley, Alfred Stieglitz, Elie Nadelman) traveled to Paris where they could meet Picasso or Matisse and visit the Louvre. Many of those who couldn't travel to Paris saw European abstract art at the Armory Show.

 ## Word Wizard

The word **abstract** comes from the Latin words *trahere* (to draw) and *ab* (from). Abstract artists think of something and then draw from it by taking its essentials.

Here are some abstract artists whose work you might see in your museum. Check off the ones you find.

- ○ **Henry Moore**
- ○ **Barbara Hepworth**
- ○ **Isamu Noguchi**
- ○ **Elie Nadelman**

Georgia O'Keeffe (1887–1986) was born in the wide open space of Sun Prairie, Wisconsin. When she was teaching in South Carolina, she pinned up her artwork on the walls of her apartment and called it her private art show. She sent some drawings to a New York friend with strict instructions not to show them to anyone. Guess what? Her friend showed them to Alfred Stieglitz, who loved them and said, "Finally a woman on paper!" That summer, O'Keeffe traveled to New York and discovered that her work was on exhibit at Stieglitz's 291 gallery—without her permission! That was the beginning of the O'Keeffe–Stieglitz relationship. She became the subject of five hundred of his photographs and his wife.

Alfred Stieglitz, *Georgia O'Keeffe,* 1918.

ART SCOOP

How is golf like painting?

To **John Marin** (1870–1953), golf and painting were alike because the fewer the strokes, the better the result. He would check the design and structure of a painting by turning it sideways and upside down to look for overall balance.

John Marin, *Movement Fifth Avenue,* 1912.

Off the Wall with

Arthur Dove
(1880–1946)

America's first abstract painter was born in Canadaigua, New York. He learned to appreciate nature from an elderly neighbor who was an artist and gave Dove his first paints and scraps of canvas.

While Dove was studying law, an art teacher saw his college yearbook cartoons and was struck by his talent. He suggested that Dove become a magazine illustrator. Against his father's wishes, Dove dropped his law studies to study art in New York. He traveled to Paris and was impressed by the Fauves' use of color and Paul Cézanne's shapes.

Later, Dove returned to New York and focused on what he is best known for: the shapes and colors of nature. His paintings lost their realistic look. He wanted to capture the spirit, or essence, of nature and the outdoors. He wanted to show things that are unseen—the heat of the sun, the growth of a tree, the force of a speedboat, or the sound of a foghorn.

"To show the pigeon would not do/and so he simply paints the coo," wrote an art critic about Dove's abstract paintings.

Did the American public like abstract art in Dove's time? No. America was involved in World War I and wanted realistic or patriotic paintings. Dove's art wasn't selling, so he turned to chicken and vegetable farming to make ends meet.

Later, he lived on a little boat for seven years. He painted, and he also created "things," his term for collages made of several materials. *The Critic* (page 21) is a thing made of newspaper, cardboard, clock spring, cord, and velvet.

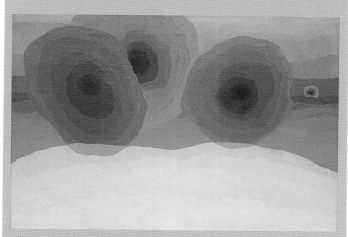

Arthur Dove, *Fog Horns*, 1929.

A   Closer Look

- Note your first impression.
- Check the background. Now check the foreground. Which takes up more space?
- How has Dove created the sound of the foghorn? (by overlapping shapes)
- In your museum, look for a painting with the feeling of noise. Check the direction of the brushstrokes.

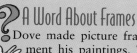

? A Word About Frames

Dove made picture frames to complement his paintings. Take a moment to look at frames in a gallery. Find a frame that is the same color as the painting it surrounds. Now find one with contrasting colors. Which do you like better?

Did you Know...

On the Floor with

Constantin Brancusi
(1876–1957)

While he was a student at the Bucharest Academy of Arts in Romania, Brancusi made such an accurate and realistic sculpture of the human body that the local medical school bought it. But his true love was abstract sculpture, and he was so determined to study it in Paris that he *walked* there all the way from Bucharest!

He spent the rest of his life in Paris, working very hard and usually alone. Like Picasso and Matisse, Brancusi admired African, ancient Greek, and Spanish sculpture for their bold geometric shapes. Brancusi reduced shapes to the smallest number of turns and curves. He is known for his simple forms that are filled with a sense of spirit. He worked in bronze, wood, marble, and other stones. He has been called the twentieth century's first abstract sculptor.

Constantin Brancusi, *The Kiss,* 1916.

A Closer Look

- What geometric shape is the sculpture?
- What does the slightly curved vertical line do?
- Check your museum for stone sculpture. Look for cuts in the surface. What do the lines create?

Moving out of the shade Brancusi was hired as an assistant in the studio of the world-famous French sculptor, Auguste Rodin, but he left after only a few weeks. He said, "Nothing grows in the shade of big trees." He did not want to copy the exterior of a person or thing the way Rodin did. He wanted to show its interior, or essence.

REVEALING REALISTS

1920–1938

If you were an artist, would you paint the real world or the imaginary world? In the 1920s and 1930s, many American artists wanted to paint the real world. They were called Realists. They wanted to create a national art about America and Americans.

What part of America did the Realists paint? Some (Edward Hopper, Reginald Marsh, Isabel Bishop) turned to the city with its scenes of loneliness. Others (Thomas Hart Benton, John Steuart Curry, Grant Wood) turned to the Midwest to show its rugged life and landscapes. A third group of Realists (Ben Shahn, Jacob Lawrence, George Tooker, Philip Evergood) used art to show the unfairness of life. They felt art should reveal the truth about the world so that the viewer might react and be inspired to change things. Regardless of their subjects, the artists were all seeing the same world outside their windows: America was in the major economic slump called the Great Depression.

Apples for sale The Great Depression in America began in 1929 with the crash of the stock market. Businesses failed, and many people lost their jobs. There was little money for food and housing. Long lines of poor and homeless people waited to be given free soup or bread. People who previously had everything they needed stood on street corners selling apples to buy secondhand clothing or wood for heat.

Uncle Sam steps in Help came from the government. It established the PWAP, the Public Works of Art Project. It lasted only six months, but provided work for thousands of artists who were asked to create paintings and murals on public buildings. PWAP was so successful that the WPA (Works Progress Administration) was set up in 1935. It supported road and bridge building, as well as the arts. Artists were paid after a committee accepted their ideas. The committee favored realistic subject matter for murals.

Walls That Speak People have painted murals on their walls since the time they lived in caves. Today, murals appear on ceilings and walls, on tombs, and in houses, office buildings, and airports. They can be painted directly on dry plaster (secco painting), on wet plaster (fresco painting), or on a canvas that is later cemented to the surface (morouflage).

Diego Rivera (1886–1957) was a well-known Mexican artist who thought his country should have a national art. He painted murals to tell about Mexico's history and to celebrate its new government. He was invited to the United States to paint murals in Detroit, San Francisco, and New York City.

ART SCOOP

Everyone you meet has a story to tell At the age of twenty-two, Jacob Lawrence (1917–2000) received art materials and twenty-six dollars a week from the WPA. Lawrence grew up in Harlem listening to his parents tell about the adventures of their trip north and how they met each other along the way. When the WPA told him to paint anything he chose, he began *The Migration Series*, sixty

paintings telling the story of the African-American migration from the South to the North.

Jacob Lawrence, *"The migrants arrived in great numbers,"* panel 40 from *The Migration Series*, 1940–41.

What is the Harlem Renaissance? Harlem is a neighborhood in New York City. *Renaissance* is a French word meaning "rebirth" or "new beginning." The Harlem Renaissance (1919–1929) was a new beginning in a neighborhood in which population had exploded as African Americans from the South journeyed to the North in search of a better life.

Harlem became the center for culture and entertainment. Jazz had already created a new awareness and appreciation of the

African-American spirit and creativity. The public's attention was now drawn to other African-American artists, such as mural painter Aaron Douglas and sculptor Augusta Savage.

Off the Wall with

Edward Hopper
(1882–1967)

"If you could say it in words, there would be no need to paint."
—Edward Hopper

Hopper showed the signs of becoming an artist when he was very young. When he was six, he turned a blackboard he had been given into an easel. Then he was given a paint box and labeled it with his named followed by the words "would be artist." Hopper grew into a tall and quiet person called Grass Hopper because of his long legs. When he studied art in New York City, his teacher told him to paint what he saw around him.

Hopper was interested in light, buildings, and figures. He felt his paintings did not tell a story, but he thought viewers could provide a story if they wanted to. Hopper is best known for giving his scenes of everyday life a sense of loneliness or isolation. To do this, he used vertical and horizontal forms, contrasting colors and patterns, body language, and empty or simple settings.

After settling in New York City, he worked unhappily making illustrations for magazines and newspapers and continued to paint in his free time. He was invited to exhibit in the Armory Show where he sold one painting. It was ten more years before he sold another!

Edward Hopper

Edward Hopper, *Room in Brooklyn*, 1932.

A Closer Look

- What is your first impression? Did you spend more time looking inside or outside the room?
- Note the space in the room: Lots of empty space creates a quiet, uneasy, or lonely feeling.
- Notice where the sunlight touches. (windowsill, flowers, floor, chair, the figure's neck)
- Look in your museum for a painting with one person. Check for shadows. See if there is a repetition of shapes like the rectangles in Hopper's work. They make the scene look very still.

ART OOPS!

It's a Win-Win One summer, Hopper went to Gloucester, Massachusetts, to paint. Jo Nivinson, whom he had met in art class, was there. She encouraged him to try painting with watercolors. She asked the Brooklyn Museum to show his works along with hers. They agreed and hung their work together. Art critics ignored her paintings and loved his! The two artists fell in love and got married. The following year, all of Hopper's paintings sold, so he was finally able to afford to paint full-time. Jo was the model for both the older and younger women in his art.

On the Mountain with

Gutzon Borglum
(1867–1941)

Mt. Rushmore.

Can you name the four presidents on Mount Rushmore? (Washington, Jefferson, Roosevelt, Lincoln) Their heads are five stories tall! The National Memorial is carved in a granite cliff in the Black Hills of South Dakota.

Gutzon worked on a large scale. One of his jobs was to sculpt a head of Lincoln out of a six-ton block of marble! The sculpture is now in the Rotunda of the Capitol in Washington, D.C.

To build up pride in America during the Great Depression, Borglum designed and supervised the memorial at Mount Rushmore. In 1927, five-foot models of the heads were lifted to the cliff's edge so workers had something to copy. They used jackhammers, drills, and dynamite on the mountain. Fourteen years later, in 1941, the year Borglum died, the memorial was completed by his son Lincoln.

Here are some other Realist artists whose work you might see in your museum. Check off the ones you find.

- ○ **Thomas Hart Benton**
- ○ **Charles Burchfield**
- ○ **Reginald Marsh**
- ○ **Isabel Bishop**
- ○ **Philip Evergood**
- ○ **Ben Shahn**
- ○ **Milton Avery**
- ○ **John Steuart Curry**
- ○ **Andrew Wyeth**
- ○ **Norman Rockwell**

ACTION ARTISTS

1940–1950s

Action artists, also called Abstract Expressionists, stress the physical act of painting. Their work has no recognizable subject matter. This style of art began in New York City after World War II. Many Action artists worked for the WPA.

How are Action artists different from other artists? They use their whole bodies to express their feelings with paint. Other artists use just hand and arm movements. Action artists are physically aggressive with their paint. Sometimes they use sticks to fling the paint toward the canvas! Also, they use very large canvases, too big to fit on an easel. Action artists roll their canvases out on the floor or tack them up on a wall.

"When I am painting, I am not aware of what I'm doing...the painting has a life of its own."
Jackson Pollock

Hans Namuth, *Jackson Pollock in Action.*

ART SCOOP

Love at second sight Patron of the arts, Peggy Guggenheim, collected and presented modern art to the public at her New York museum called Art of This Century. When she first saw Jackson Pollock's work, she said, "Awful. Dreadful, isn't it?" But when her friend, Dutch artist Piet Mondrian, told her it was the most interesting work he had seen in America, she looked longer and changed her mind! She liked Pollock's work so much she asked him to do four solo shows at the museum and a mural for the hall of her apartment. The mural is pictured opposite.

Off the Wall with

Jackson Pollock
(1912–1956)

When Pollock was twelve, his mother was a cook at an Arizona ranch. While she worked, he explored Indian ruins and discovered Navajo sand paintings, which are made by dripping colored sand onto the desert ground. Later, Pollock became known for dripping and flinging house and car paint onto a canvas. After the first layer dried, he would use brushes and sticks to draw darker and thicker lines. Exploring other ways of making a painting, Pollock once even pushed a tricycle covered with paint over the canvas!

Move over, chicks Jackson Pollock joined two of his brothers in New York to study art with Thomas Hart Benton, a Midwestern Realist known for his murals. Benton and Pollock became good friends. In fact, Pollock's first studio, Jack's Shack, was a former chicken coop on Benton's property on the island of Martha's Vineyard, Massachusetts.

Jackson Pollock, *Mural*, 1943.

A Closer Look

• What is your first impression of this painting? What did you notice? Try to keep in mind that this work is huge—twenty feet long and eight feet high!

• Look for repeated vertical lines. Check for circular shapes.

• Try to follow one color in the painting.

• Look around your museum for a busy painting. Make up a title for the work. How was the paint applied?

Off the Wall with

Franz Kline
(1910–1962)

In the 1940s, while his friends were experimenting with Surrealism and other European styles, Franz Kline was a part-time decorator and illustrator.

Kline's life changed the day he visited the studio of his friend and mentor Willem de Kooning. By coincidence, de Kooning was using a projector to enlarge some of Kline's own sketches and doodles! The sight of his own work looking so large inspired Kline to change his style from small, realistic sketches or doodles to huge canvases of Abstract Expressionism.

He began projecting his drawings onto gigantic canvases tacked up on the wall. After examining the enlarged sketch, he painted with commercial black paint, which he bought by the gallon. He worked at night under strong spotlights. He said, "The white was just as important." To create the white in his paintings, he left the canvas unpainted.

Franz Kline, *Turin,* 1960.

Kline is known for his simple, strong, black brushstrokes. His new style of painting inspired others to use fewer colors and simple shapes or symbols.

A Closer Look

- Look at the painting for a few moments. Did your eye and mind settle in one area? Where? Or did you keep moving about the painting?
- Focus on just white shapes made by the unpainted surface.
- Look in your museum for paintings with fat brushstrokes. Are the edges solid or frayed? Are the strokes fast or slow?

A field of color Another group of Abstract Expressionists recorded their feelings in a quiet or spiritual way. They Did you Know... soaked their canvases with fields of color. They were called Color Field painters. They invited the viewer to enter into the color and have an emotional experience in their color portraits.

Off the Wall with

Helen Frankenthaler
(1928–)

After attending Bennington College, Frankenthaler studied art under Hans Hofmann as did many other avant-garde artists. Frankenthaler married Abstract Expressionist Robert Motherwell (1915–1991). They lived, worked, and exhibited in New York.

Frankenthaler worked with huge canvases on the floor and let the color and the texture of the paint itself become the subject of her compositions. She often created brushless paintings! How? She poured paint onto the canvas. The colors would run into each other and overlap, staining or dyeing the cloth. The flowing shapes and movement in Frankenthaler's work remind viewers of wind or water. She is known for her "portraits of color" and for the feeling of nature in her paintings.

Helen Frankenthaler, *Flood,* 1967.

A Closer Look

• What is your first impression? How does this painting compare to Kline's?
• Do you miss seeing brush-strokes?
• What would you title this? Frankenthaler calls it *Flood.*
• Look in your museum for an eight-foot canvas. How was the paint applied? Can you see through the layers?

Where the action is Have you noticed less discussion of European artists and more about American artists? By the middle of the twentieth century, the center of the art world had moved from Europe to America. New York City was where the art action was taking place.

A word about sculptors Sculptors have always used a variety of natural materials to express themselves. The modern world gave them new materials and tools: stacks of crushed cars (John Chamberlain), personal and small collections in decorated boxes (Joseph Cornell), trays of "junk" sprayed black and piled into twenty-foot walls (Louise Nevelson), and welded iron and steel (David Smith). Check your museum for modern materials used in sculpture.

Off the Ceiling with

Alexander Calder
(1898–1976)

Calder's mother was an artist, and his father and grandfather were sculptors. He studied engineering and art. When he was twenty-eight, he paid for a trip to Paris by painting the ship he sailed on!

Calder was a friendly, well-liked man with a sense of humor. He divided his time between France and America. He is well known for his wire sculptures and his miniature circus. But he is probably most famous for his graceful and abstract mobiles and stabiles, which are found in public places—airports, office buildings, company headquarters, and museums—all over the world.

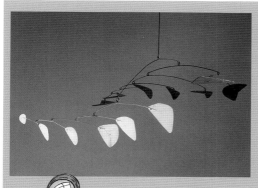

Alexander Calder,
*Model for East
Building Mobile,* 1972.

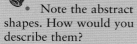

- Note the abstract shapes. How would you describe them?
- Imagine that one shape is removed. How does that change the balance?
- If your museum does not have a mobile, select a painting with shapes you like. How would you arrange the shapes into a mobile?

Word Wizard

Marcel Duchamp combined the words **motive** and **motion** to name Calder's hanging sculptures "mobiles." At first, Calder's mobiles were powered by a crank or by electricity. Later, mobiles were stirred only by the air around them. Did you have one when you were young?

"**Stabile**" was the name Jean Arp gave Calder's floor sculptures. They stayed put while the viewer moved around them!

ART SCOOP

Mobiles and earlobes? Peggy Guggenheim loved modern art. She wore an unusual pair of earrings to one party at her museum. One earring was made by Calder and the other was made by Yves Tanguy, a Surrealist painter! Guggenheim wanted to show she had no favorites!

Here are some other Abstract Expressionsts whose work you might see in your museum. Check off the ones you find.

- ○ **Willem de Kooning**
- ○ **Robert Motherwell**
- ○ **Philip Guston**
- ○ **Adolph Gottlieb**
- ○ **Mark Tobey**
- ○ **Mark Rothko**
- ○ **Clyfford Still**

Popular Pop Artists

Mid 1950s–1960s

What comes to mind when you see the word *pop?* Dad? Bang? Popular? Popsicle?

Pop Art is about images taken from daily life, such as comic strips, a picture of a hamburger or a celebrity, or even items from the trash! Pop Art's colors are strong and lively like the advertisements in magazines or television. Colors are not blended but have hard edges when they meet another color. Pop artists usually signed their work on the back because they didn't want their presence in the painting.

Where did the name come from? The term "Pop Art" was used by art critics to describe a collage made by Richard Hamilton in England in 1956. The word "pop" was painted on a lollipop in the collage.

Going global Popular music and art went international in the fifties and sixties. Bill Haley's tune *Rock Around the Clock* rocked all the way around the globe. Elvis Presley was the subject of Pop Art paintings by Andy Warhol and British artist Peter Blake. Bringing together popular music and popular art, Blake even created album covers for Elvis.

Did you Know...

Change the channel! Do you ignore commercials on TV or switch channels when they come on? Andy Warhol (1928–1987) might have done the same thing. He felt there were too many images bombarding the public. He wanted everyone to stop and notice them and learn to think about them in a new way. To help people do this, he would single out a picture and repeat it hundreds of times on the same canvas! Among the images he focused on were a soup can, a gory photograph, and a picture of a celebrity.

Off the Wall with

Robert Rauschenberg
(1925–)

Rauschenberg was always searching for new ways to express himself. "A picture is like the real world if the real world is in it," he said. He walked the streets looking for things to put in his artworks, which he called *combine paintings*. In them, he mixed different materials and techniques, creating combinations of painting and sculpture. Sometimes he also included photographs to convey his social or political views.

A   **Closer Look**

- What is the first thing you saw? Hunt for other familiar objects.
- Which parts look real?
- Which parts look abstract?
- Look in your museum for a combination of two materials in one artwork.

Robert Rauschenberg, *Tracer*, 1963.

Love and war at the museum   *Tracer* won an international prize in 1963. It isn't a combine, but if it were, what else do you think Rauschenberg would have added— maybe an eagle or a parking meter?

ART SCOOP

A man of many talents Rauschenberg did not limit himself to painting. He also wrote and choreographed a ballet called *Pelican*. He danced in it wearing a parachute and roller skates!

On the Floor with

Claes Oldenburg
(1929–)

Oldenburg was a newspaper reporter, but he quit this job to do what he really loved—sculpture.

Oldenburg created sculptures of things we might find in our homes: tools, hamburgers, a toaster, or a tube of toothpaste. His first exhibitions included poems he wrote, which he painted several feet tall and placed next to his sculptures.

As time went on, Oldenburg's sculptures grew softer. He made them out of cloth, plastic, and vinyl (stuffed with kapok). They also grew larger. He made a baked potato as big as a car! His wife helped him in the beginning. Later, things got out of hand—literally—like when he made a forty-five-foot clothespin! Soon he had to have his designs completed at a factory.

Claes Oldenburg, *Floor Cake (Giant Piece of Cake)*, 1962.

- Look for triangles.
- How many layers do you see? (five)
- Look around your museum for food in art. How would you depict your favorite food?

A Closer Look

Look before you eat! Oldenburg enjoyed the shape of the food he saw and ate. He saw architecture and geometry everywhere: the beauty of three round stories found in a hamburger or in a triangular cone holding a spherical scoop of ice cream. Hungry? How about a nine-foot piece of cake?

Wrapped for takeout George Segal (1924–2000) was a sculptor of everyday scenes. He had people strike a pose, and then wrapped them in strips of wet plaster-fabric. When the

plaster dried, he carefully cut the wrappings away in sections to release his model. Next, he reassembled the sections to recreate hollow life-size human forms. Finally, he placed his people in an environment he set up with props like bus seats or counters.

George Segal, *Portrait of Sidney Janis with Mondrian Painting,* 1967.

What else was popular in the Sixties? It rhymes with pop. Op art. Op is short for optical, which refers to eyes. Op artists use wavy lines and patterns. The close position of the lines and colors shocks our vision. The result is so stimulating to the eye that it causes a physical reaction. Op art images move or jiggle. They can even irritate your eye or give you a headache! A former Bauhaus teacher, Josef Albers, was the leader in Op art. He wanted three things in art: color, shape, and order. Op art certainly has order!

Off the Wall with

Bridget Riley
(1931–)

When she worked in advertising, Riley used the style of painting with tiny dots that is best known in the work of Post-Impressionist Georges Seurat. She studied his ideas of how one color may react or seem to vibrate when placed next to a different color. Interested in movement and energy, she also studied the Futurist's works.

Riley distorted shapes to make them play optical tricks, and painted thousands of parallel but curved black lines on her canvases. She is known for paintings that assault the eye, are filled with energy, and have life and movement.

Bridget Riley

Bridget Riley,
Current, 1965.

A   Closer Look

• What was your first impression? Did your head go up and down?
• Where was the first "wave"?
• Try to follow one particular line. Does it remind you of a roller-coaster ride or of skiing?
• Look for other paintings that give your eyes a "ride."

Did you Know...

And the winner is. . . In 1968, Riley was the first woman to receive the International Prize for Painting from the Venice Biennial, a major international art exhibition. Rauschenberg received the same prize in 1964 for his painting on page 59.

Here are some other Pop and Op artists whose work you might see in your museum. Check off the ones you find.

○ **James Rosenquist**
○ **Tom Wesselmann**
○ **Richard Stankiewicz**
○ **Marisol**

○ **Lee Bontecou**
○ **Jim Dine**
○ **Edward Kienholz**
○ **Victor Vasarely**

MARVELOUS MINIMALISTS

1960s

What do you get when you remove people, feelings, and things from painting and sculpture? You get the bare essentials, the minimal ingredients of art: color, line, and shape. Minimalism was "Art-as-art-as-art," wrote Ad Reinhardt, an artist and newspaper reporter.

Minimalism was probably a response to the Action artists, who made their feelings visible on canvas. Or it could have offered relief from the confusion and conflict in the social climate of the sixties: the Vietnam War and the battles for civil rights and women's rights.

> **ABCs OF MINIMAL ART**
> **A**rt that's
> **B**arren and
> **C**ool with
> **s**culpture as the main subject

 How did the artists like their label? The name *Minimalism* was made popular by British philosopher Richard Wolheim. He used it to describe works with the smallest number of ingredients and with no evidence of the artist's emotion. The artists and sculptors didn't like the name but it helped the public refer to their works.

Here are some Minimalists whose work you might see in your museum. Check off the ones you find.

- ○ **Ellsworth Kelly**
- ○ **Agnes Martin**
- ○ **Robert Ryman**
- ○ **Donald Judd**
- ○ **George Baer**
- ○ **Brice Marden**
- ○ **Eva Hess**

On the Floor with

Sol LeWitt

(1928–)

LeWitt first studied drawing before turning to the three-dimensional world of architecture. He worked for world-famous architect I. M. Pei. His continued interest in architecture is revealed in his art.

"Only ideas can be works of art," said LeWitt. He felt that after the artist creates the idea—which he thought was the most important thing in a work of art—he could then give it to others to make. He is known for his ideas of order and simplicity in his painting and sculpture.

Painting the environment Once he knows what he wants, LeWitt sends or faxes his instructions for an artwork to a museum. The art is created there, according to his directions. His art becomes more than a painting or sculpture—it becomes an environment! A sample of his instructions for a wall painting is: "Within six inch squares, draw straight lines edge to edge using yellow, red." It took an artistic mind to figure it out!

Sol LeWitt, *Three Cubes (Angle),* 1969.

A   Closer Look

- What is your first impression? Look around the work. Note how the angles change.
- Imagine one sentence of LeWitt's instructions for creating this sculpture.
- Look for another piece of sculpture and note how it changes as you walk around it.

Detached art is when an artist has the idea and writes instructions for others to do it. Do you think this concept could apply to homework?

Did you Know...

Off the Wall with

Dan Flavin
(1933–1996)

Flavin is known for his colorful and bright light sculptures. He is one of the few self-taught artists in this book, and the only one who works with the subject of electricity.

Flavin uses fluorescent lights, those long tubes of light you can find in any hardware store. Usually fluorescents are used on the ceilings of supermarkets, factories, and schools—not in museums as sculptures! Does this remind you of Duchamp's ready-mades?

Watts up? To create a composition, Flavin made many decisions. He had to decide whether the sculpture would go on the floor or the wall, what thickness fluorescent

tubes to use, what colors and shapes they should be, the number of lights, and their arrangement, spacing, and wattage. Then he had an electrician actually make the piece…detached art!

Flavin's sculptures produce color and light that spill onto the area where they are exhibited. They change the environment. His art flows to the viewer in a gentle shower of light.

A Closer Look

- What does the sculpture look like to you? Lights? A building? A person?
- Note the reflection on the floor.
- What hardware items would you gather to make a sculpture?

Dan Flavin, *"monument" for V. Tatlin,* 1969.

Word Wizard

Rock around the desk One day in 1852, Sir George Stokes, an English scientist, was sitting at his desk. He noticed a glow surrounding a sample of the mineral fluorspar as it rested on his desktop. He called it **"fluorescent."** Fluorspar, or fluorite, is used in making fluorescent lights.

Activities

Hunts

If interest in the museum visit begins to fade, try reviving it with a hunt!

Material hunt: Look for and make a list of at least six different materials you find in various paintings and sculptures (oil, cloth, watercolor, etc.).

Subject hunt: Find a painting that has at least three subjects. For example, *The Red Studio* (page 19) is about the color red, studio space, and art.

Music hunt: Select two favorite paintings. Go to the library and learn about the kind of music popular when the paintings were made.

Questions to Ask Yourself When Viewing Modern Art

- What is this work about?
- What else is happening?
- What do I see that makes me think that?
- Why did the artist choose to create this work in this way?
- What was the artist trying to say?

Making Art

Monochrome: On a sunny day, gather a poster-board, one crayon or marker, and a bicycle wheel. Prop the wheel near the posterboard so it casts a shadow. Trace the shadow and color it. You'll have a monochrome work of art!

Chance collage: You'll need one large piece of white paper, several pieces of colored paper, scissors, and paste. Keeping in mind the work of Dadaist Jean Arp, carefully tear the colored paper and let the pieces fall freely onto the large piece of paper. Arrange them slightly to suit your eye. Paste them in place and sign your name!

Memory collage: Think of an experience you've had or a place you've visited. Write down some words that describe it. Look through magazines and newspapers for these words. Cut them out and paste them on a poster. The text can remain alone or be filled in with photographs you've taken, or pictures you cut out or draw.

Writing

Shapescape: Look out the window. Find three shapes. Now look for a shape that is repeated two or more times. Is it in the foreground, middleground, or background? Instead of using paint to depict what you see, use words to describe it.

The Hopper effect: Take a walk with a friend in your town. Look for a vacant bench, an empty space, a closed shop, or a solitary person in a quiet setting. Check the light and shadows falling around the scene, and notice the sense of quietness. Go home and write a paragraph picture describing your silent encounter.

Dadaist poetry: Cut out ten to twenty large-size words from a magazine. Place them in front of you. Turn the radio on to a very high volume. Now read the words in a poetic way!

Recipes

Mrs. Drew's Warhol Meatloaf

Andy Warhol was famous for his *200 Cans of Tomato Soup* painting. Here is one way to use one can of Campbell's tomato soup.

> *1 pound hamburger*
> *1 roll Ritz crackers, crushed*
> *1 egg*
> *half package dehydrated onion soup*
> *2 shakes ketchup*
> *salt and pepper*
> *1 strip bacon*
> *1 can Campbell's tomato soup*

Combine the first six ingredients with your hands and form the mixture into a brick. Put into a loaf pan, and place a strip of bacon on top. Pour the undiluted Campbell's tomato soup on top! Bake for one hour at 350°.

Minimalist Cheese Sticks

With their emphasis on simplicity in shape and color, the minimalists probably would have loved this hot appetizer.

1 can grated parmesan cheese, poured onto a large plate
1 stick butter, melted
1 loaf white bread, crusts removed

Cut each slice of bread into thirds from top to bottom. Paint both sides of each bread "stick" with the melted butter. Place bread, one side at a time, in grated cheese until cheese adheres. Arrange bread on a cookie sheet. Broil until golden. Flip and broil the other side. Be careful: They burn easily!

CREDITS

cover Salvador Dali, *The Persistence of Memory,* 1931. Oil on canvas, 9½ X 13" (24.1 x 33 cm). The Museum of Modern Art, New York. Given anonymously. Photograph © 2000 The Museum of Modern Art, NY. © 2000 Foundation Gala-Salvador Dali/VEGAP/Artists Rights Society (ARS), New York.

PAGE

2 Rembrandt van Rijn, *Artist in His Studio,* ca. 1629. Oil on panel, 9¾ x 12½" (24.8 x 31.7 cm). Zoe Oliver Sherman Collection. Given in memory of Lillie Oliver Poor. Courtesy Museum of Fine Arts, Boston.

7 Andrew Wyeth, *Christina's World,* 1948. Tempera on gessoed panel, 32¼ x 47¾" (81.9 x 121.3 cm). The Museum of Modern Art, New York. Purchase. Photograph © 2000 The Museum of Modern Art, NY.

8 Norman Rockwell, *The Connoisseur.* Printed by permission of the Norman Rockwell Family Trust. © The Norman Rockwell Family Trust.

10 Hans Hofmann, *Goliath,* 1960. Oil on canvas, 84⅛ x 60" (214 x 152 cm). University of California, Berkeley Art Museum; gift of the artist. Photograph by Benjamin Blackwell. © Estate of Hans Hofmann/Licensed by VAGA, New York, NY.

11 Qi Zhaijia, *Winter Landscape,* dated 1678. Hanging scroll, ink on paper, 82½ x 28" (212 x 72 cm). Collection of Roy and Marilyn Papp, photo courtesy the Phoenix Art Museum.

12 Stuart Davis, *Hot Still Scape for Six Colors—7th Avenue Style,* 1940. Oil on canvas, 36 x 45" (92.5 x 115.6 cm). Courtesy the Museum of Fine Arts, Boston. Gift of the William H. Lane Foundation and the M. & M. Karolik Collection, by exchange. © Estate of Stuart Davis/Licensed by VAGA, New York, NY.

14 David Smith, *Cubi XVII,* 1963. Polished stainless steel, 107¾ x 64⅜ x 38⅛" (277 x 165.5 x 98.6 cm). Dallas Museum of Art, The Eugene and Margaret McDermott Art Fund, Inc. 1965.32.MCD. © Estate of David Smith/Licensed by VAGA, New York, NY.

16 Morris Louis, *Delta Gamma,* ca. 1960. Oil, miscible acrylic (magna) on canvas, 10¾ x 150⅝" (27.6 x 386.8 cm). Courtesy the Museum of Fine Arts, Boston. Anonymous gift.

17 Constantin Brancusi, *The Kiss,* 1916. Limestone, 23 x 13 x 10" (58 x 33 x 25 cm). Philadelphia Museum of Art: The Louise and Walter Arensberg Collection. Photo by: Graydon Wood, 1994. © 2000 Artists Rights Society (ARS), New York/ADAGP, Paris.

18 *Exterior View of the 69th Regiment Armory, 1913.* Walt Kuhn, Kuhn Family papers, and Armory Show records, Archives of American Art, Smithsonian Institution.

19 Marcel Duchamp, *Nude Descending a Staircase, No. 2,* 1912. Oil on canvas, 57⅞ x 35⅛" (147 x 89.2 cm). Philadelphia Museum of Art: The Louise and Walter Arensberg Collection. Photo: Graydon Wood, 1994. © 2000 Artists Rights Society (ARS), New York/ADAGP, Paris/Estate of Marcel Duchamp.

19 Henri Matisse, *The Red Studio,* 1911. Oil on canvas, 71¼ x 7'2¼" (191 x 219.1 cm). The Museum of Modern Art, New York. Simon Guggenheim Fund. Photo © 2000 The Museum of Modern Art. © 2000 Succession H. Matisse, Paris/Artists Rights Society (ARS), New York.

21 Arthur Dove, *The Critic,* 1925. Collage of paper, newspaper, fabric, cord, and broken glass, 19¾x 13¼ x 4¾" (50.2 x 33.7 x 12.1 cm). Collection of Whitney Museum of American Art. Purchase, with funds from the Historic Art Association of the Whitney Museum of American Art, Mr. and Mrs. Morton L. Janklow, the Howard and Jean Lipman Foundation, Inc., and Hannelore Schulhof 76.9 Photo © 2000 Whitney Museum of American Art.

21 Alfred Stieglitz, *The Steerage,* 1907. Chloride print, 4¼ x 3½" (11 x 9.2 cm). The Alfred Stieglitz Collection, 1949.705. Photograph © 2000, The Art Institute of Chicago, All Rights Reserved.

23 Ernst Ludwig Kirchner, *Street Scene: Two Ladies in the Street,* 1922. Woodcut, printed in color, 27¾ x 15" (70.6 x 38 cm). The Museum of Modern Art, New York. Purchase. Photograph © 2000 The Museum of Modern Art, NY.

25 Wassily Kandinsky, *Panel for Edwin R. Campbell No. 3,* 1914. Oil on canvas, 64 x 36¼" (162.5 x 91.2 cm). The Museum of Modern Art, New York. Mrs. Simon Guggenheim Fund. Photo © 2000 The Museum of Modern Art. © 2000 Artists Rights Society (ARS), New York/ADAGP, Paris.

27 *Picasso in front of* Guernica, *July 1937.* Courtesy Magnum Photos, Inc. © 1937 David Seymour.

28 Pablo Picasso, *Three Musicians,* 1921. Oil on canvas, 6'7" x 7'3¾" (200.7 x 222.9 cm). The Museum of Modern Art, New York. Mrs. Simon Guggenheim Fund. Photograph © 2000 The Museum of Modern Art, NY. © 2000 Estate of Pablo Picasso/Artists Rights Society (ARS), New York.

29 Jacques Lipchitz, *Man With a Guitar,* 1915. Limestone, 38¼ x 10½ x 7¾" (97.2 x 26.7 x 19.5 cm). The Museum of Modern Art, New York. Mrs. Simon Guggenheim Fund (by exchange). Photograph © 2000 The Museum of Modern Art, NY. © Estate of Jacques Lipchitz/Licensed by VAGA, New York, NY/Marlborough Gallery, NY.

30 Giacomo Balla, *Dynamism of a Dog on a Leash,* 1912. Oil on canvas, 35⅜ x 43½" (90 x 110 cm). Bequest of A. Conger Goodyear and Gift of George F. Goodyear, 1964. Albright-Knox Art Gallery, Buffalo, NY.

31 Joseph Stella, *Battle of Lights, Coney Island, Mardi Gras,* 1913–1914. Oil on canvas, 6'4" x 7'1" (195.2 x 215 cm). Yale University Art Gallery. Bequest of Dorothea Dreier to the Collection Société Anonyme.

32 Coney Island Steeplechase Park. Photo courtesy Coney Island USA.
33 Umberto Boccioni, *Unique Forms of Continuity in Space,* 1913. Bronze (cast 1931), 43⅞ x 34⅞ x 15¾" (111.2 x 88.5 x 40 cm). The Museum of Modern Art, New York. Acquired through the Lillie P. Bliss Bequest. Photograph © 2000 The Museum of Modern Art, NY.
35 Marcel Duchamp, *Bicycle Wheel,* 1951 (3rd version, after lost original of 1913. Assemblage: metal wheel mounted on painted wooden stool, overall: 50½ x 25½ x 16⅝" (128.3 x 63.8 x 42 cm). The Museum of Modern Art, New York. The Sidney and Harriet Janis Collection. Photograph © 2000 The Museum of Modern Art, NY. © 2000 Artists Rights Society (ARS), New York/ADAGP, Paris/Estate of Marcel Duchamp.
36 Jean Arp, *Growth,* 1938. Bronze, 31¼ x 12½ x 8" (79 x 32 x 20 cm). Philadelphia Museum of Art: Bequest of Curt Valentin. © 2000 Artists Rights Society (ARS), New York/ADAGP, Paris.
38 Salvador Dali, *The Persistence of Memory,* 1931. Oil on canvas, 9½ x 13" (24.1 x 33 cm). The Museum of Modern Art, New York. Given anonymously. Photograph © 2000 The Museum of Modern Art, NY. © 2000 Foundation Gala-Salvador Dali/VEGAP/Artists Rights Society (ARS), New York.
40 Joan Miró, *The Harlequin's Carnival,* 1924–25. Oil on canvas, 26 x 36⅝" (66 x 93 cm). Room of Contemporary Art Fund, 1940. Collection Albright-Knox Art Gallery, Buffalo, NY. © 2000 Artists Rights Society (ARS), New York/ADAGP, Paris.
41 Alberto Giacometti, *Dog,* 1951. Bronze. © 2000 Artists Rights Society (ARS), New York/ADAGP, Paris.
43 Alfred Steiglitz, *Georgia O'Keeffe,* 1918. The Metropolitan Museum of Art, Gift of David A. Schulte, 1928.
43 John Marin, *Movement: Fifth Avenue,* 1912. Watercolor, with traces of black crayon, over charcoal, 16¾ x 13¾" (42.8 x 34.8 cm). The Alfred Stieglitz Collection, 1949.554. Photograph by Kathleen Culbert-Aguilar, Chicago. Photograph © 2000, The Art Institute of Chicago, All Rights Reserved. © 2000 Estate of John Marin/Artists Rights Society (ARS), New York.
45 Arthur Dove, *Fog Horns,* 1929. Oil on canvas, 18 x 26" (46 x 66 cm). Courtesy Colorado Springs Fine Arts Center.
46 Constantin Brancusi, *The Kiss,* 1916. Limestone, 23 x 13 x 10" (58 x 33 x 25 cm). Philadelphia Museum of Art: The Louise and Walter Arensberg Collection. Photo by: Graydon Wood, 1994. © 2000 Artists Rights Society (ARS), New York/ADAGP, Paris.
48 Jacob Lawrence, *"The migrants arrived in great numbers,"* panel 40 from *The Migration Series,* 1940–41. Tempera on gesso on composition board, 12 x 18" (30.5 x 45.7 cm). The Museum of Modern Art, New York. Gift of Mrs. David M. Levy. Photograph © 2000 The Museum of Modern Art, NY.
50 Edward Hopper, *Room in Brooklyn,* 1932. Oil on canvas, 29⅛ x 34" (74 x 86.4 cm). The Hayden Collection, 35.66. Courtesy Museum of Fine Arts, Boston. Reproduced with permission. ©2000 Museum of Fine Arts, Boston. All rights reserved.
51 *Mt. Rushmore.* Photograph courtesy the South Dakota Department of Tourism.
52 Hans Namuth, *Jackson Pollock in Action.* ©Hans Namuth Estate. Collection Center for Creative Photography, The University of Arizona.
53 Jackson Pollock, *Mural,* 1943. Oil on canvas, 19'10" x 8'1¼" (6 x 1 m). The University of Iowa Museum of Art, Gift of Peggy Guggenheim (1956.6) © 1959 The University of Iowa Museum of Art, All Rights Reserved. Photo: Ecco Hart. © 2000 Pollock-Krasner Foundation/Artists Rights Society (ARS), New York.
54 Franz Kline, *Turin,* 1960. Oil on canvas, 80⅜ x 95½" (204.1 x 242.6 cm). The Nelson-Atkins Museum of Art, Kansas City, Missouri (Gift of Mrs. Alfred B. Clark through the Friends of Art). © 2000 The Franz Kline Estate/Artists Rights Society (ARS), New York.
55 Helen Frankenthaler, *Flood,* 1967. Synthetic polymer on canvas, 124 x 140" (315 x 355.6 cm). Collection of Whitney Museum of American Art. Purchase, with funds from the Friends of the Whitney Museum of American Art 68.12 Photo © 2000 Whitney Museum of American Art.
57 Alexander Calder, *Model for East Building Mobile,* 1972. Painted aluminum and steel wire, 11⅜ x 27¼" (29 x 69 cm). National Gallery of Art, Washington, DC. Gift of the Collection Committee. © 2000 Estate of Alexander Calder/Artists Rights Society (ARS), New York.
59 Robert Rauschenberg, *Tracer,* 1963. Oil and silkscreen on canvas, 84⅛ x 60" (213.7 x 152.4 cm). The Nelson-Atkins Museum of Art, Kansas City, Missouri (Purchase). © Robert Rauschenberg/Licensed by VAGA, New York, NY.
60 Claes Oldenburg, *Floor Cake (Giant Piece of Cake),* 1962. Synthetic polymer paint and latex on canvas filled with foam rubber and cardboard boxes, 58⅜ x 9'6¼" x 58⅜" (148.2 x 290.2 x 148.2 cm). The Museum of Modern Art, New York. Gift of Philip Johnson. Photograph © 2000 The Museum of Modern Art, NY.
61 George Segal, *Portrait of Sidney Janis with Mondrian Painting,* 1967. Plaster figure with Mondrian's "Composition" 1933, on an easel, 69⅞ x 56¼ x 27¼" (177.3 x 142.8 x 69.1 cm). The Museum of Modern Art, New York. The Sidney and Harriet Janis Collection. Photograph © 2000 The Museum of Modern Art, NY. © The George and Helen Segal Foundation/Licensed by VAGA, New York, NY.
62 Bridget Riley, *Current,* 1965. Synthetic polymer paint on composition board, 58⅜ x 58⅞" (148.1 x 149.3 cm). The Museum of Modern Art, New York. Philip Johnson Fund. Photograph © 2000 The Museum of Modern Art, NY.
64 Sol LeWitt, *Three Cubes (Angle),* 1969. (160 x 305 x 305 cm). Courtesy Louisiana Museum of Modern Art, Humlebaek, Denmark. © 2000 Sol LeWitt/Artists Rights Society (ARS), New York.
65 Dan Flavin, *"monument" for V. Tatlin,* 1969. Fluorescent tubes and fixtures, 96⁵⁄₁₆ x 32⁵⁄₁₆ x 4¾" (244 x 82 x 12 cm). Collection Walker Art Center, Minneapolis. Gift of Leo Castelli Gallery, 1981. © 2000 Estate of Dan Flavin/Artists Rights Society (ARS), New York.